GTD® With The Bullet Journal®

Using your favorite tool with the world's best productivity method

By Derek Reinhard

Text Copyright© 2020 Next Step Communications, LLC

All Rights Reserved

Legal Stuff: Disclaimers and Credits

1. This book is one of an ongoing series. Each book focuses on how to use David Allen's Getting Things Done® (GTD®) system by customizing a particular organizing/productivity tool, and then showing how to step through the various GTD system workflows. Because each of these books show various ways to use GTD, there is some common material. However, each book produces unique content and instructions for using that particular book's focus tool with the GTD system.

2. These books are for entertainment and informational purposes. They cannot be construed in any way, explicitly or implicitly, to resemble professional advice. The reader assumes all responsibility if they choose to follow any instructions in these books. No success is guaranteed or warranted. The author is not employed by nor does he represent any companies mentioned except Next Step Communications, LLC. All views are his own.

3. The links and other external references were current at the time of publication. The author makes every effort to keep them current. Clicking on some of the links and then subsequently making a purchase may result in the author receiving a small commission.

4. Getting Things Done®, GTD®, GTD Weekly Review®, Natural Planning Model®, and Mind Like Water® are registered trademarks of and/or copyrighted by the David Allen Company. Bullet Journal®, The Bullet Journal Notebook, BuJo®, The Bullet Journal Method are registered trademarks of and/or copyrighted by Ryder Carroll and/or Lightcage, LLC. They own all the rights to their respective brands and intellectual property. For clarity of print and reading, the ® and ™ superscripts are not used though still refer to the registered trademarks as stated.

Table of Contents

INTRODUCTION 6
    The Power of the BuJo Notebook and Method 8
    The Power and Flexibility of GTD 8

GTD OVERVIEW 9
    The Essential Rules of GTD 10
    The Importance of Being Ruthless... 11

BULLET JOURNAL OVERVIEW 14
    The BuJo Basics 14
    The BuJo Layout and Key 15
    It's All About the Index! 15
    The BuJo "Flow" 15

PUTTING IT ALL TOGETHER 17
    GTD with the BuJo Notebook 17
    How Do I Get Started Setting Up My GTD BuJo Notebook?............ 17
    How Do I Set Up My Horizon Pages? 23
    Can I Start Adding Page Numbers to My Index, Yet?....... 23
    What Is The "Flow" of Using My GTD BuJo Notebook?.... 26
    How Do I Set Up My Daily Log? 28

START LIVING GTD WITH YOUR BUJO NOTEBOOK 29
    Now How Do I Set Up My Projects? 29
    Start Worry-Free Living (Well, Worry-Free Productivity Anyway)! 30
    A Brief Note Where the BuJo Notebook Doesn't Play So Well With GTD 31

STAYING ON TRACK... 33

GETTING BACK ON TRACK.. 34

ADDITIONAL TOOLS AND ACCESSORIES 35

DOES THIS WORK WITHOUT THE ACTUAL BULLET JOURNAL NOTEBOOK?	36
WHAT ABOUT THE GTD 43 "TICKLER FILE" FOLDERS?	37
SOME FINAL THOUGHTS	38
Glossary of Terms (NOT Comprehensive)	39
HELPFUL RESOURCES	41
THANK YOU's	42
ABOUT THE AUTHOR	42

INTRODUCTION

Since I'm a let's-get-to-it kind of guy, I'd like to keep this introduction short and get to showing you how to increase your confidence in your own productivity. I expect you are reading this book because you like Getting Things Done (GTD) or The Bullet Journal (BuJo) Method, or you're curious about (maybe even frantic for) optimizing your productivity with different tools. Whatever your motivation, I am confident you will find here an easy explanation and step-by-step instructions to get up and running with your own personalized notebook and action plan for getting the most out of using the GTD method in a BuJo Notebook.

NOTE: This book is NOT a shortcut to understanding the GTD system or the BuJo Method.

In this book, I assume you are familiar with the BuJo and, more importantly, that you have worked your way through "Getting Things Done" (https://gtd-with.com/GTDBook) by David Allen. There is much you can learn about the BuJo Method in Ryder Carrol's book (https://gtd-with.com/BuJoMethod) and website (https://gtd-with.com/BulletJournal), and from all the enthusiastic BuJo community members. But to get the most out of GTD with the BuJo, you need to be well acquainted with GTD to appreciate and apply the essential points I will make as we work through setting up your BuJo Notebook (https://gtd-with.com/BuJo) for GTD, and then building your own GTD rhythm and style.

To start, the Bullet Journal Method is a crazy popular way of journaling while organizing your day and tasks. It is all about capturing your creativity, feelings, observations, events, planning and day-to-day tasks in a nice looking, minimalist notebook form. David Allen's Getting Things Done (GTD) system continues to rule the productivity world. GTD is about just that, getting things done; it focuses on effective planning and doing your most important tasks at the optimum time and place (even if the task is to relax). You can do this confidently because you know that it is the best time to be doing that one thing. "Mind Like Water" as David Allen puts it. The GTD system doesn't prescribe what tools you use to help you be productive (well, okay, it is rather folder-intensive for managing physical items like paper); still, at its heart, GTD describes some essential rules and patterns of behavior to help you be your most productive self, anytime and anywhere. And, at the same time, it shows you how to move things forward that are most important to you right now, all based on the values and priorities you set for yourself.

I had the idea for this book series about 2 years ago after I'd been using a BuJo Notebook to organize my life around David Allen's GTD. I discovered a sweet spot for those of us who really enjoy (or need to enjoy) the slower, reflective use of pen and paper, which is where the BuJo Method is strongest. Match this with the efficiency of knowing what the best "next action to take" is, which is the hallmark of GTD, and I think you have a rich, satisfying way to focus on your life and what you want to accomplish, all in notebook form. This book has both step-by-step instructions on how to "shape" the tool to GTD while keeping the creative power of BuJo—all without compromising the unique productivity power of GTD. NOTE: As you can see already, both Getting Things Done and The Bullet Journal Method have their own unique terms and concepts. I've listed some of the most essential in the Glossary; although this is not a comprehensive list, but it contains the most essential terms I use in this book.

The Power of the BuJo Notebook and Method

The BuJo Method is a hugely popular journaling method. Taking a minimalist approach to creative organizing and journaling (it's an empty dot grid book for goodness sake!), the BuJo Method answers the challenge of keeping your daily thoughts and activities in an accessible, sequential format without the waste of empty pages that a calendar-based journal organizer would create. A typical organizer calendar boxes you into the same size of space for each day (usually smaller for weekends), rather than giving you the power and flexibility to fill as much or as little space as you need each day, day after day, to put your thoughts, feelings and creativity in order.

The Power and Flexibility of GTD

GTD is one of the most popular productivity systems on the planet. The simplicity of GTD makes it powerful. But the simplicity also makes it easy to morph into something less productive because of cutting corners. GTD is "tool agnostic", meaning it can be implemented using most any organizing tool you want, electronic or paper based. This enables flexibility and personalization for individual users—there is no right or wrong way to manage your productivity with digital and/or physical tools and still stay true to the GTD method. This means the BuJo Notebook is a perfect complement to the GTD.

GTD OVERVIEW

Getting Things Done is an organizing and execution system that puts all your "work" in a place where you can get it done when, where, and how it best suits you. Key to the system is clearing your inboxes (physical, electronic, and mental) and planning/organizing the results so you are free and confident to identify and work on what is best for you, moment-by-moment, day-by-day, looking weeks and even years ahead.

The GTD methodology centers on questions like "What is my next task?" and "What is the best thing to do with this time I find I have right now?". GTD breaks big, important, desired results/objectives ("Horizons" in GTD terms), into a planned series of next actions. Rather than spending time creating a To Do list each day (which indirectly fills up your day with tasks that may or may not be the most important things to get done that day), GTD focuses on reviewing and scanning. When you don't have an appointment (a time-bound commitment), you are scanning for best actions to do at that given time and situation. There is flexibility in your calendar (it's amazing how much blank space shows up when you don't fill them with To Do's!). And in those open blocks of time are opportunities you have missed to be your most productive self. But this doesn't mean you can let your time and choices go off on their own; spending your time planning for results is essential.

When you do GTD's Natural Planning Model, you define why a project is important, what the outcome will look like, and then create a list of next actions or tasks. Then you put the next "Next Action" for each of your projects to move forward into buckets appropriate for the task. David Allen calls these buckets "Contexts" – this is an important concept to grasp firmly in GTD: Contexts (one type of "Collection" in the BuJo Method) are where you create lists of activities from many different projects which can be done in a certain setting (examples include "At Home", "At Work", "Computer", "Phone Calls", and so on).

The Essential Rules of GTD

"Commitment" is an important GTD concept which is different from Prefer or Want or even Need to do. In order to get the full effect of the GTD system, it is absolutely essential to maintain the "hard edges" between the Must Do of appointments, which are calendar-bound, and the Must of a commitment to complete a project because the project is important to you and your life, but doesn't always have a required deadline. Notice that that second list of Must Do's isn't calendar-bound the way that work and appointments have a due-on-this-day date. The importance of GTD and getting the most out of your goals and commitments is to shape your tool, NOT the methodology. This is different from customizing GTD to reflect your life. For example, if ever I retire, there will no longer be an "At Work" context.

Another customization of GTD could be creating your GTD 43 folders (more on this later) electronically rather using paper file folders. You will always have Commitments, Projects, and Contexts, and you will always have some form of 43 folders for GTD, or you really aren't doing GTD. These are what I see as unchangeable or essential aspects of the GTD system. The primary activity in the GTD flow, after emptying your inboxes and doing the appropriate planning, is scanning and reviewing. Scan, scan, scan (or review, review, review) to maximize productivity. If you are not focusing on a commitment, then you scan for what Context you are in. Once you identify which Context(s) you are in at the moment, narrow down your list of Next Actions in that Context based on how much time you have available, what your energy level is, and what is a priority for you.

You almost always have at least one Next Task to do in any one of your Contexts—once you identify your Context (or Contexts, such as you can be both "At Home" and "Computer" and, if you want to separate it out, "Email"), then you apply the other rules of time available, energy level, and priority. Doing this exercise consistently, moment-by-moment, helps identify your best Next Action or Task.

Because the flow of GTD and being productive involves inboxes, projects, next tasks, and contexts, then it is essential that you are confident of where you need to put things. Having a method for consistently putting things in their appropriate place makes you confident that you will be able to find them when you need to. In the field of Knowledge Management, these two concepts are "Placeability" and "Findability".

For example, with my system of setting up my BuJo for GTD, I know my Context list starts on a given page (and if I forget, the Table of Contents, a key BuJo resource, will tell me where my Contexts are). That way, I will ALWAYS know how to get to that information when I need it. For placeability, I know to put the Next Action of each of my projects into their appropriate Context so I know confidently that what is important to me is also easy for me to find and act on.

When I show you how to set up your notebook, you will be able to choose where all these items go so that you too will have confidence in the reliability of your system of placing and finding.

The Importance of Being Ruthless

To tap into the power and wisdom of GTD, you must give up a degree of "I know best for me". I read in many blogs, and forums, and I hear in conversations how someone "does GTD, except I do this instead ", when what they change or do differently is exactly one of the things David Allen says is core to the power of GTD—those essential, unchangeable rules that makes the GTD method well, the GTD method that works its productivity magic.

Here is my list of the three unchangeable rules for "doing GTD":

Essential GTD Rule #1

Maintain the hard edges between the types or categories of things you encounter. David Allen sees seven primary categories. This is where I think most people lose their productivity edge—they do not keep a ruthlessly hard edge between these categories which then leads to inconsistent placeability and findability, which then leads to a loss of confidence in their system, or at least a slowing down in their productivity—and probably a half-effective workaround. The types of things needing hard edges:

1. Projects List (Horizon 1 in GTD, and one type of Collection in the BuJo Method)

2. Project Support Material for each item in your project list

3. Calendar actions and information – It only goes on the calendar if it is an appointment to keep, or a task which MUST be done that day/time, or information to be remembered at a specific time—such as birthdays and anniversaries

4. Next Actions Lists (in your Context buckets or Context Collections)

5. "Waiting For" List

6. Reference Material

7. "Someday/Maybe" List – These are projects or areas of interest I might want to do something with someday, but I do NOT want to spend any more time thinking about them now except to write them down in this list to be referred to later. I now have the freedom to ignore them and refer to them while I am doing my periodic review and planning

The BuJo Notebook can be good for managing all the "hard edge" categories, except project support material and reference material (which we will also discuss managing later).

Essential GTD Rule #2

Scan, scan, scan to keep the flow –identify your most important next task by evaluating where you are (in this order): Context, Time Available, Energy Level, Priorities. For example, I'm at home with an hour before someone is going to call me; I'm feeling full of energy and my areas of focus (Horizon 2) include putting more of my home in order. I have a project (commitment) to clean up my workshop. In my "At Home" Context, one of my Next Actions includes organizing my workbench. I can do that in an hour and get cleaned up before my phone call.

Essential GTD Rule #3

Keep clearing your inboxes. GTD has a workflow for organizing every item that comes into your life—through inboxes, in baskets, the mailbox, your ideas, someone else's ideas/tasks, etc. You don't need to have empty inboxes at the end of each day, but keeping on top of what comes at you by turning them into what they are (the GTD Workflow) will make your weekly review and daily planning go more smoothly and allow you to focus on acting rather than on managing your inboxes.

In my opinion, I think all the rest of GTD productivity hangs on these three "rules". Incorporating them into your journaling life will go a long way to being satisfied with your productivity and reaching your goals.

BULLET JOURNAL OVERVIEW

"Journal" along with its Rapid Logging method (bullet-like symbols and speed) is the heart of the BuJo Method. The BuJo Notebook is a place where creativity and organizing coexist. There are any number of variations on the Bullet Journal Method. Ryder Carrol even includes community-developed additions in his book on The Bullet Journal Method—one of these additions is the Calendex (https://gtd-with.com/Calendex) which I have adapted for GTD with BuJo use and will share with you when we start setting up our Future Logs. While there is a codified BuJo method, it is flexible in the ways it can be used. For example, along with the Calendex, there are other useful techniques and styles created by the BuJo community that include additional rapid logging symbols, page number chains to thread topics together when their content isn't on consecutive pages (or not even in the same notebook), etc..

The BuJo Basics

One of the greatest features of the BuJo Method is that it uses a physical book in the way we were taught to read a book: front-to-back (or back-to-front if your language goes in that direction), page by page. The BuJo Method is used in such a way as to progress your journal in subsequent pages without having to leave large blank spaces or even entire pages which is what a journal with dated pages often does.

The "Rapid Logging" technique lets you enter and then see at a glance the status of your tasks, events, notes, thoughts, and feelings (and anything else that may catch your attention, such as the weather, sports scores, and the like). These are the sorts of things that make your journal memorable, useful, and uniquely yours.

The BuJo is highly customizable as you use it around the practice of Rapid Logging and what are called "Collections" (Groups of Logs for your Projects as well as Monthly, Daily, and

Future appointments and activities). On the BuJo website, there are many examples of how to organize and display these logs. In this book, I'll share a few techniques for depicting your Logs as well as explaining why I chose the ones I use for my GTD practice.

The BuJo Layout and Key

The Bullet Journal Notebook is a customized version of the hardcover Leuchtturm1917 dot grid book (https://gtd-with.com/Leuchtturm1917). The Bullet Journal notebook (https://gtd-with.com/BuJo) comes with instructions and tips, unnumbered pages for the Index, and pages 1-4 with the header "Future Log".

This setup will be our springboard into building your Bullet Journal Notebook to empower your Getting Things Done life.

Remember: Index, Future Log, open pages for Getting Things Done

It's All About the Index!

In The BuJo Method, the Index is the hub for identifying where you keep information as well as guiding you where to place new information (the 3 different book marks are also helpful for getting to your most used and referred to areas in your BuJo—more on that later).

The beauty of the BuJo Method is how it helps you efficiently use the Notebook like a book – page by page. The BuJo Method enables you to fill in your notebook, front-to-back, as well as confidently jumping to the information you need at any moment.

The BuJo "Flow"

As in GTD, the BuJo emphasizes continuous review to be sure you're staying focused and not missing any important information or events. Your Index and Collections keep you organized for placing and finding information.

There are many ways people personalize how they use a BuJo Notebook. Of course, they complete tasks and track their days, but they also add color (literally) to their days. As with any planner, the Bujo Notebook follows a regular sequence or "Flow". Here is a general summary of instructions from the BuJo Notebook (There is an in-depth description, and an inspiring read, in Ryder Carroll's book, The Bullet Journal Method https://gtd-with.com/BuJoMethod):

1. At the end of the current month, lay out the upcoming month with appointments and events

2. Enter the current Monthly Log page number to your Index

3. Lay out the upcoming day on two opposite pages—appointments and events on the left page and tasks on the right page

4. Set up the Future Log (pages 1-4 in the BuJo Notebook) by dividing the pages so each space on the page can be used to capture things that need to be scheduled beyond the next month

5. Use the index for capturing the page numbers of other collections you create, whether they are drawings or project notes or other topics

6. Keep the pattern going for each day and month; create pages and capture the page number in the Index; create, capture, repeat <grin>

(If you want the in-depth explanation, please read The Bullet Journal Method as well as visit the BuJo website to understand the day-to-day use of a BuJo Notebook).

PUTTING IT ALL TOGETHER

The primary parts of Getting Things Done with the Bullet Journal Notebook are BuJo's rapid logging symbols, the Future Log (I use a modified Calendex approach to the Future Log), and a combination of the Index and the bookmarks to quickly access the power of GTD's Horizons, Planning, and Contexts.

GTD with the BuJo Notebook

Setting up your BuJo Notebook with the Getting Things Done system will involve three steps:

1) Getting the Notebook physically ready to use

2) Customizing the first 20 pages or so to align with the GTD method (the actual number of pages you use will depend on how much artwork you like to put in as well as the length of your personal GTD Horizon statements, and if you want to create the Monthly Logs ahead of time)

3) Enter or migrate existing appointments and project information

How Do I Get Started Setting Up My GTD BuJo Notebook?

1. <u>Getting your BuJo Notebook physically ready</u> (do as much or as little as you like with his step; it won't impact creating your GTD BuJo)

   a) Iron the three bookmark ribbons with low heat to take out creases. They will lay flatter and more neatly inside your notebook and where they stick out below the pages when your journal is set on a desk (Ryder Carroll has a nice tutorial on breaking in a new BuJo at <u>http://gtd-with.com/BreakInBuJoNotebook</u>)

   b) Put the notebook on a hard, flat surface like a desk, table or counter and go page by page and fully open each one.

As you go, carefully separate any pages where glue may have bled between them near the binding. This will help your journal lay flatter when you're working with it

c) Get a ruler or other straight edge to help draw neat lines wherever you want ; I use a folding ruler (http://gtd-with.com/FoldingRuler) which I can keep in the back pocket of my notebook

2. Build your Table of Contents/Index first, but you're NOT going to add page numbers yet! We'll fill in those later in the setup process.
After the Future Log, the first few pages of my BuJo contains those things that won't change much: my GTD Horizon Statements. Next, I note in my Index those things that change or get added to regularly (Master Project List (or Horizon 1 Commitments), Contexts, and my "Someday/Maybe" lists).

a) Draw a vertical line on the left side of your first two Index pages; place the line about ¾" (2 cm) from the left to make a column on those first two pages. Later, after creating

some of your pages, you will come back and put their page numbers in the column (see photo for the way I marked that page number column)

I will show you later how I create a full 12-month Calendex (four columns per page) for my Future Log on pages 1-3, and use the fourth page to capture Special/Observance days.

b) Go down the first Index page creating section headers and their individual contents (refer to the next photo of my latest BuJo Notebook setup)

    i. <u>Horizons</u> – From Purpose to Commitments

    Horizon 5 – Purpose and Principles

    Horizon 4 – Vision and Mission

    Horizon 3 – Goals and Objectives

    Horizon 2 – Areas of Focus & Accountability

    Horizon 1 – Commitments/Master Project List

If you want, you can split your Horizon 1 commitments like I did or keep them combined. I split out my Horizon 1 commitments so there are two different Master Project Lists, one for my personal project commitments and the other for Horizon 1 projects for work. If you keep all your commitments in one list, you can stop with "*5. Horizon 1*"

    ii. <u>Contexts</u> – Next Actions and Tasks

    - Calls
    - Emails
    - Computer/Smartphone
    - Errands
    - At Home
    - At Work

- Agendas - This page is actually a table of contents for agenda pages I create in my notebook for different people and meetings

- Must Read/Review

iii. Label what is located at your bookmarks; for me, my bookmarks are:

Black – Weekly Log
Gray – Today Log
White – Waiting For (Back pages)

3. <u>Build your Someday/Maybe Table of Contents</u> on the second page of your Index

a) Projects

Personal
Work (optional)

b) Perhaps of Interest *

Food
Books to Read
Movies/TV
Weekend Trips/Getaways
Children/Grandchildren
Seminars/Training
Websites
Spouse Might Like
Other Reading
Music

*This list is adapted from GTD in the "Organizing: Setting up the right buckets" section.

In the photo, you can see how my two Index pages look in my own GTD BuJo Notebook.

4. Set Up Your Future Log

Your Future Log will take up pages 1-4 (to match the BuJo Notebook Index). I use the Calendex design, but I use rapid logging symbols for appointments and events and then create a Monthly Log where each of those items is spelled out.

I begin by going down the side of each Future Log page, numbering 1 through 31. These will guide me as I complete each monthly column, marking out the weeks.

The next photo is what my new Calendex looks like. Page 1-3 are monthly columns, 4 months per page, and the 4th page has a full year showing recurring events such as birthdays and anniversaries. In the photo you can see pages 3 and 4; the monthly columns on the left page are the last four months of my current Calendex (in this case, February-May, 2021) and the right-hand page is my year of observance and special days.

I've drawn a horizontal line at the end of each week in each of the month columns—my weeks start on Monday so the horizontal line has Sunday above the line and Monday after the line. You can see that I've hashed out the last days if a month has less than 31 days. I use the space at the bottom of each month for appointments and tasks I must accomplish sometime that month.

How Do I Set Up My Horizon Pages?

As you complete your Horizon statements, put a page number in your index for each Horizon. If you set up your Index like I did, then page 5 will be for your GTD Horizon 5 – Purpose and Principles. If you've not gone through the exercise of defining your Horizons (5 down to 2), then please review that section of the GTD book. Once you've formulated these statements, come back and copy them to your BuJo Notebook on the appropriate pages. David Allen is keen on neatness while explaining how to setup your GTD system. I found a nice, inexpensive label maker (http://gtd-with.com/LabelMaker) to use when I want those kinds of neat headers in my BuJo (such as Horizon headings).

Can I Start Adding Page Numbers to My Index, Yet?

Yes, after you've entered the content for your Horizon statements. My Horizon 5 and 4 statements are briefer than the others, so they are both on page 5. Next are my Horizon 3 and 2 statements, each taking up a full page. My page numbers down the column for those Horizons are pages 5, 5, 6, and 7. Notice in the photo that I put these page numbers in the center of the column. That's because this content is pretty much set—this is what my life and being are about, at least for the next 12-24 months. I don't expect to be adding more page numbers for these.

When it comes to Horizon 1 and all my Contexts, this is more active content—I put their page numbers on the left-hand edge of the page number column in the Index. I do that because, if it turns out that I am particularly busy going through my projects, I may need another page for my Horizon 1 Master Project List. The next Master Project List page number will go next to the original one in the Index.

In my Contexts, if I go through a lot of phone calls and emails, for instance, I may need to start another page for those Contexts. That page number will go next to the first one (and, if all the Next Actions on the original page are completed, that original page number can get the Rapid Logging "X" for Completed).

Now, go to the next empty page in your notebook and label it Horizon 1 or Master Project List to capture all your current commitments that need to be planned and executed (not the ones you want to do or ought to do—just the ones you WILL do). If applicable, do the same for your Horizon 1 List for Work. For me, my Personal and my non-profit Master Project Lists are on page 8 and 9.

Do the same again for each of the Contexts or Next Actions and Tasks lists—one per page. Look at the photo and see the completed page numbering. Also notice how I added the content found at each of the different colored book markers (this is optional because you'll quickly remember what content you are using for each of your bookmarks). For me, the black bookmark is my current Weekly Log , the grey one is my current Daily Log, and the white bookmark is my "Waiting For" List.

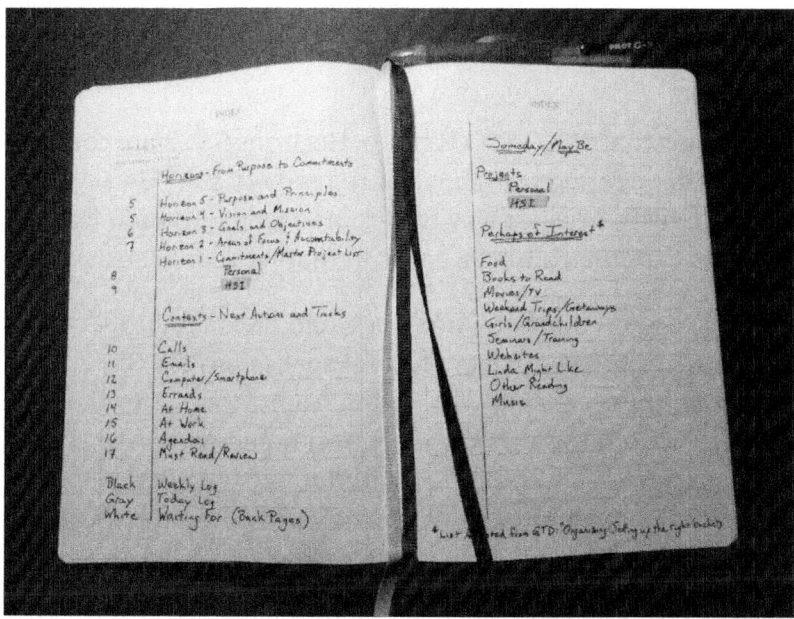

Also, notice that I do not yet have any pages for my Someday/Maybe items. When I identify my first project that I <u>might</u> want to do, I start a Someday/Maybe Project list and put that page number next to either Personal or HSI (my nonprofit). The same goes if I come across food, books, websites, things my grandchildren may like, etc.—Start a page labeled with that Someday/Maybe list and put that page number in the Someday/Maybe index page.

One handy thing for me is that I can always remember that my Context lists start on page 10, so I can go straight there when I am scanning for the most important next thing to do in my current situation. Of course, when pages multiply for a Context, there is always the Index to get me where I need to be. I also thread page numbers (putting the follow-on page number next to the current page number to show where that page's additional material is located).

What Is The "Flow" of Using My GTD BuJo Notebook?

> *"The way to get started is to quit talking and begin doing."*
> – Walt Disney

Now that your Index is setup, Horizons 5 to 2 are completed and page numbering started, you are ready to start Getting Things Done! I think the easiest way to kick off a new GTD BuJo Notebook is to start with the coming week, by creating your Weekly Log.

1. Go to your first open page and divide it into 4 rows, do the same on the next page. These 8 spaces are for the 7 days of next week (my planning week goes from Monday to Sunday). I prefer to have 4 rows on pages opposite each other so I can see my entire week without flipping pages. NOTE: If you want to have your week showing on two opposite pages, and you find you need to leave a page blank to do that, then immediately put that blank page's number on the next open line in your Horizon 1 Master Project List. That way, the next time you need to commit to a project, you will already have that page number next in your project list and an open page ready for planning!

2. In seven of those rows in your Weekly Log, label each space with the day of the week and date. The eighth space is good for focus items based on your Horizon 2 statement, inspirational thoughts, or notes about the week.

3. Mark this week with a bookmark since you'll be referring to it in planning and adding appointments as you live through this week. You can mark the page number for this Weekly Log in your Future Log/Calendex as well. I put the page number of my Weekly Log on the right-hand end of the corresponding Monday in my Calendex.

4. Now, using your current calendar tool, go to your Future Log/Calendex and copy any appointments in the coming week and

for the rest of the month. Because the columns are narrow in the Calendex, use Rapid Logging signifiers to designate appointments, events, tasks due on given dates. I use the upside-down V for appointments. This is explained on page 244 in the back of the BuJo Notebook. How do I know what each of those symbols for appointments, tasks, and events are in my Future Log? I create a Monthly Log.

    a. In my Calendex, I draw a small open square at the top of each column below the month name. When I need to capture my first appointment of a given month, I put the page number of my next open page in that small square and start my Monthly Log. You can see this setup in the photo of my Calendex (The green highlights are my regular Mondays I have off while the blue highlights are holiday days off)

    b. When you start a Monthly Log, divide the page into three rows (I do that so I can estimate days of the month); the 1st through the 10th of the month in the top row, the 11th through the 20th for the middle row, and the 21st to the end of that month in the bottom row. You can use your own way of tracking your future appointments. I just find this the simplest (though sometimes messy if I have a lot of appointments across one or two days)—sometimes in my Monthly Log, some of the appointments aren't in chronological order. At least they are grouped together so I will see them when I scan. I also add any observance and special days from that page in my Future Log.

c. If you are okay with blank pages because you want your Monthly Logs in consecutive order, you can create each month's Log and put their consecutive page numbers in the small square at the top of each month's column in your Calendex. I've tried this both ways. I prefer creating the Monthly Log as it is needed when I record my first appointment/commitment date for that month because it won't leave a bunch of blank Monthly Log pages in a row (like a normal calendar journal).

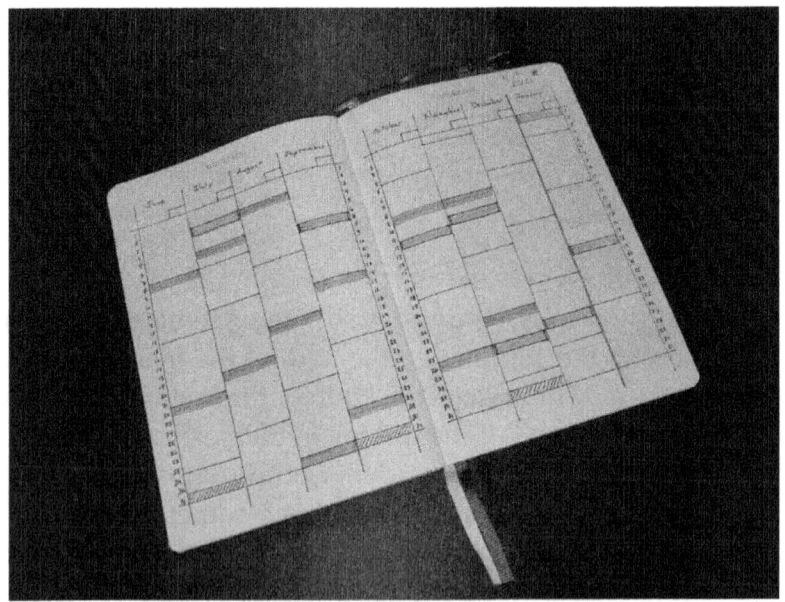

How Do I Set Up My Daily Log?

Now that your Weekly Log for the next week is filled in, go to the next fresh page and label it "Today" and enter the day of the week and the date. Mark this "Today" with another bookmark (I use Gray for Today—just because it rhymes lol). You can record the Today page number on that date in your Weekly Log, and even in your Future Log if ever you need to easily locate that day's page sometime in the future.

START LIVING GTD WITH YOUR BUJO NOTEBOOK

You now know your current situation! Well, at least you know the appointments you have for the coming week. The key to start living GTD with BuJo is that, when you are not actually in an appointment, you have a choice to make. You can be:

1. Preparing for your next appointment,
2. Planning work for a project,
3. Scanning your current Context(s) for Next Tasks/Actions, or
4. Processing your inboxes

Whichever you discern is most important for you at that moment in time, given your time available right then, your energy level, and your sense of priorities.

You are now set up to live with a "Mind Like Water" which David Allen describes is the state of confidence you experience when you have a trustworthy planning and tracking system.

Now How Do I Set Up My Projects?

One benefit of using journaling is that the act of writing can bring you pause and clarity—you can decide whether you really want to or ought to commit to something.

1. When committing to a project, write it down in your Horizon 1 Master Project List; this signals your brain that it is a matter of your personal integrity that you will start this immediately AND finish it. If you already have a page number you put there from your Weekly planning, go to that page and write the project name at the top of that page. If there isn't a page number available, after you write the project name in your Master Project List, go to the next open page, add the project name and then go back to put that page number next to the project name in your Horizon 1, Master Project List. If you like, you could draw a thin column at the left side of your Horizon 1 page to set off the page numbers for each project, like I showed you for the page number column on the Index pages

2. On that project page (and using more if needed), go through the Why, What, and How of GTD's Natural Planning Model.

3. When you identify at least one Next Task in that project, add it to the appropriate Context (Yes, you're right, in my GTD with BuJo Notebook they start at page 10)

Go through those three steps for every project you are currently committed to. Again, the psychology of writing these out long-hand will make you pause to assess which projects you really are and should be committed to.

Start Worry-Free Living (Well, Worry-Free Productivity Anyway)!

The focus of the GTD method is on your near-term commitments and effectively processing everything that comes to your various inboxes and has your attention. Your weekly and daily planning, and moment-by-moment mindfulness of your context is where you live most. You review your Horizon 1, Master Project List weekly to confirm you are moving your work forward (recording Next Actions in the appropriate Context list).

Horizons 2 and 3 have to do with personal accountability and the sorts of objectives those projects are moving you toward. You could review those Horizons every 6 to 12 months. Because GTD leaves you to sort out your farther Horizons (4 and 5 are about your principles and values). If you've worked hard to clarify those, you can review and revise them every 2 to 5 years. I do go back and review my 2 through 5 Horizons on New Year's Day each year as an exercise in reminding me and grounding me in the bigger picture of my life. Now let's get back to our day-to-day life.

After your Weekly Planning is completed, and your day is setup in your BuJo Notebook, it just comes down to either managing your attention on what commitment you have now, or focusing on identifying your current Context and then choosing the Next Action or Task that fits your situation.

Of course, it isn't that easy since we seem to be bombarded (or at least our various inboxes are) with new information, ideas, tasks, hopes, wishes, and emergencies. This is where GTD can take you to places of calm productivity. The BuJo Notebook, set up for the GTD method, can help you get and stay there.

A Brief Note Where the BuJo Notebook Doesn't Play So Well With GTD

I think you would agree that it took a bit of time and effort to set up your BuJo Notebook in the GTD fashion, didn't it? Your GTD with BuJo notebook is something you can be proud of and enjoy as you fill it going forward. It can even bring you a sense of joy and satisfaction as you plan and track your accomplishments. You can even make it reflect your personality by embellishing it with art, doodles, thoughts, and dreams.

Because it is a blank notebook where you plan and track, it's not something you want to rush through and keep replacing. That's why I think the BuJo Notebook doesn't support being a high-volume inbox or note-taking space. If your livelihood, hobbies, or even your personality, generates a lot of new thoughts and material, you may find yourself migrating to new BuJo Notebooks more often than you care to.

To avoid needing to set up and migrate my BuJo Notebook material too soon and before you feel you've wrung out all the beautiful productivity you can from that notebook, you want to consider having a separate notebook to be your "inbox/idea box". It can be a physical or digital inbox/idea box to record detailed notes, tuck in content to process, etc. It is something that will continue to help you keep the hard edges on your stuff. It will also keep your GTD with BuJo notebook focused on tracking and logging. As part of your daily/weekly planning, you can take the material in your inbox/idea box notebook and transform it into whatever it needs to become: Projects go into either your Master

Project or Someday/Maybe Project List, Tasks in your Context lists, information for future reference, contacts, etc.

To save time transcribing, you could also make a note on the relevant project page in your GTD with BuJo notebook to point to the page in your inbox/idea box notebook that has the material relevant to that project. For example, on the project page in your GTD with BuJo notebook, you can put "A-23" which points to page 23 in your "A" notebook that you are using as your inbox/idea box. This enables you to enjoy your GTD with BuJo Notebook longer while going through basic, cheaper notebooks (https://gtd-with.com/dotnotebooks).

While I was doing my day job the other day, teleworking this time, and I glanced down at my desktop. I realized I had the perfect photo opportunity to show you how this two-notebook approach works in real time. Notice to the left of my laptop is my GTD with BuJo notebook ready to place or find something if needed. To the right (I am righthanded) is my Inbox/Idea Box notebook where I am capturing tasks for future transfer, notes from meetings, etc. I have one pen for my GTD with BuJo notebook and another for the cheaper notebook. I hope that photo helps (and, no kidding, this was a real situation on a real day—welcome to what my work life looks like).

STAYING ON TRACK

It takes deliberate effort to create a good habit; that includes using GTD and your BuJo notebook. There are two key activities to help you get things done consistently:

First, having a set time each day to create your "Today" page. Some people do this planning before going to bed while others prefer creating and planning their day after they get up. Because I'm an early bird (and not very interested in exerting my brain right before bed), I do my "Today" planning first thing in the morning.

Second, and probably most important, is to NOT create lists for the day. Obviously, if a task must be done by a certain time/date, you need to schedule time to work on it, just like an appointment. Otherwise, you scan, scan, scan the environment for the context you are in and act accordingly.

Scanning is the most challenging habit for me: monitoring my situation, recognizing when I am in "free time" and going to Contexts. My tendency is to either think up something to do regarding what is on my mind at that moment (even if I've not captured it as a project or task) or, worse, reacting to whatever is in my inbox. One of the essential skills in GTD that has supercharged my productivity is to get out of my inbox , not working out of my inbox. In fact, regularly processing everything in my inbox so that it is empty a lot of the time has probably been the most liberating accomplishment I've ever done. David Allen calls this process in GTD, "The Workflow" (https://gtd-with.com/GTDWorkflow)—it is taking each thing that comes at you and turning it into what it is: something to file, or trash, put it off (defer it on purpose), hand it off to someone else, put it in a queue to create a project or a maybe-project, etc.

An overfull, unprocessed inbox wears on your time, even effects your mental wellbeing worrying about the known and unknown in it. There are many books, seminars, blogs, etc. about managing your inbox and the impact an unruly inbox has on you. I've added a brief list of sites, books, and tools in the Resources chapter which I hope you'll find helpful in building habits in general, as well as specifically managing your inbox.

GETTING BACK ON TRACK

The steps for getting back on track are much like setting up and getting started. It's an adventure to explore the reasons why you weren't using your GTD BuJo Notebook to its best effect. Perhaps you are overreaching the number of commitments you are making (a favorite flaw of mine); you get to thinking, "I need to do that" or saying, "Yes, I'll do that for you". Pretty soon, you have so many commitments in your Horizon 1 Master Project List that you start losing track of your tasks or you can clearly see you don't have enough time to commit to every one of them.

As I said before, the inbox is a place many people get bogged down in, you're not alone. Perhaps you see every email as an urgent item to read and respond to quickly, even if you're only in the Cc line. Or maybe your inbox never really got emptied so it has information buried in it, tasks that are about to go very badly, or just looks like a huge, intimidating pile of stress-making emails.

Then again, perhaps it really is just a matter of not making the time to plan each day and each week; things end up piling up again and you have to fall back on your old practices of firefighting the hottest issue that pops up closest to you.

Getting your inbox to zero is an essential condition to Getting Things Done (and I would argue, essential to a comfortable life in general). Just as I described in the list of what I think are the unchangeable GTD rules, you really cannot fully benefit from using the Getting Things Done system until you have made the time to process each item in your inboxes.

It's that important for getting on track and staying on track.

ADDITIONAL TOOLS AND ACCESSORIES

The Back Pocket

A bonus to the BuJo Notebook is the accordion pocket on the inside back cover. For me, it is my one-stop storage place for GTD planning as well as holding key reference material. What's inside my back pocket right now? A folding ruler I use for drawing lines in my Weekly and Daily Logs, a book of postage stamps, and a local commuter bus schedule until I get used to the new neighborhood my wife and I moved to recently. I also have a set of GTD cards (https://gtd-with.com/gtdcards) that include instructions for The Workflow, the Natural Planning Model, the Weekly Review, and other aids to continue Getting Things Done.

Pen Loops and Pens

A small but useful accessory I'm using is a pen loop to attach to my GTD with BuJo notebook. It helps keep a pen close by. There are several sources for narrow pen loops (http://gtd-with.com/NarrowPenLoops) , as well as pen loops for larger barreled pens (http://gtd-with.com/LargePenLoops). I use gel ink pens which usually have a larger diameter ink barrel, like the fine-tipped Pilot G2 (http://gtd-with.com/PilotG2). I love the look and feel of writing with gel pens. Please not that there are two possible inconveniences to watch out for: first, not every pen loop is large enough for your pen (thus my finding the larger pen loop) and, second, depending on the quality of your gel pen, the ink dries more slowly after you write. It can smudge or transfer to the opposite page if you close your notebook before it is finished drying. With the Pilot G2, this rarely happens to me but is something to watch out for.

DOES THIS WORK WITHOUT THE ACTUAL BULLET JOURNAL NOTEBOOK?

As I mentioned, the Bullet Journal Notebook is a customized version of the hardcover Leuchtturm1917 (I remember backing its development when Ryder was originally crowdfunding it). The BuJo Notebook features that are missing from the plain Leuchtturm1917 are the Bullet Key on the inside front cover, Tips on the first page, and an introduction to bullet journaling on the last nine pages. Additionally, the Leuctturm1917 notebook only has two thin bookmarks, black and grey, and only two pages for a table of contents/index.

The Bullet Journal Notebook has 244 blank pages (including the Future Log) while the plain Leuchtturm1917 has 249. You could also try the softcover version of the Leuchtturm1917 (https://gtd-with.com/SoftLeuctturm1917), but it only has 123 pages, including the table of contents/index. I used this softcover notebook for my last GTD with BuJo notebook and I went about 5 months with my normal use. I am now switching to the full Bullet Journal Notebook which should last me the next 8-10 months, perhaps longer, depending on how well I also use my inbox/idea box notebook.

All that said, the only thing I do differently with a plain Leuchtturm1917 has to do with the missing white bookmark. I still use the black bookmark for my Weekly Log and the grey one for my Daily Log. Without the white bookmark, I just need to manually flip to the back of the notebook to review my "Waiting For" list.

WHAT ABOUT THE GTD 43 "TICKLER FILE" FOLDERS?

As explained in Getting Things Done, these folders are where you can put physical reminders of things to do in the next 31 days and future months. In my 43 folders are things like prescription refill reminders, UPS receipts (to later confirm online that the package was delivered), recurring weekend checklists, etc. Every morning when I create my Daily Log, I look at the contents of that day's "tickler" folder and put an action note on the "Today" page I am creating. Soon I may explore other ways to manage these items, such as digital 43 folders with notes scanned or typed in. But for now, since I prefer the tactile experience (like writing in my BuJo), I will physically file items, cards, and other reminders into my 43 folders.

An Additional Tickler: The "Weekly Frame"

I don't recall where I came across this, but at some point I needed to set up a weekly rhythm of recurring activities. I created a single page with Monday-through-Sunday columns where I could enter things I want to do daily or regularly each week. I have exercise scheduled on most days, video conference reading with my grandson, personal reading time blocks, and the like. I printed this weekly frame and attached it to the front fly leaf page (that stiff page) of my notebook. In my daily planning, I refer to my tickler folder and put in that day's appointments in my Daily Log ("Today" page). I then look at the weekly frame and transfer that day's recurring tasks and "appointments". If you like the Weekly Frame idea but might not like attaching it to your GTD BuJo notebook, you might consider putting a copy in your tickler files so it turns up each day.

SOME FINAL THOUGHTS

I hope this book and its instructions were helpful for setting up and running your own GTD with BuJo notebook. I have worked this way for years and found it very satisfying and productive. When it comes to the Bullet Journal, I am less a creative person and more a list person. I will take time to draw the "Today" label in different styles for each Daily Log. This makes for some fun variety and entertainment to start the day and get my creative juices flowing. Other than that and drawing the occasional mind map while taking notes, my standard practice is to simply cross off tasks and put a big diagonal line across a day or a project page when it is complete. Rather than making a journal to look back on, my notebooks are tools which often get pulped after I'm done. However, the role your notebook plays for you as you get things done is entirely up to you! What works for you? What satisfies you as you navigate your personal productivity and life? For sure, you can be as creative and winsome as you like, even making your BuJo into a keepsake that you can reference, reminisce and, enjoy in the future.

Take your own path for making your journal uniquely yours—add color, free-hand drawings, template shapes (https://gtd-with.com/templates), decorative self-adhering tape (https://gtd-with.com/journaltape), colorful, multi-shape stickers (https://gtd-with.com/Stickers), whatever you like. This is your personal way of being creative while being productive using your Getting Things Done with Bullet Journal Notebook!

Glossary of Terms (NOT Comprehensive)

Daily Log (BuJo)	This is your "Today" calendar in GTD; appointments and "due today" work/tasks
Calendex (BuJo)	A format of the BuJo's "Future Log" developed by an enthusiastic member of the Bullet Journal Method community
Collection (BuJo)	Any list of related items. In GTD collections would be Contexts (lists of "Next Actions" associated with a place/situation), Horizon 1 Projects, etc.
Context (GTD)	A list of work "buckets" where next actions and tasks are collected, depending on a given situation. For example, At Home, At Work, Computer, Errands, Calls, etc.
Future Log (BuJo)	A list or table of scheduled appointments, events, and tasks happening further out than the current month. Probably most useful in monthly groupings
Horizon (GTD)	Statements you craft about your life from various levels of detail. The highest Horizon, Horizon 5, is about your purpose and principles; down to "ground level" Horizon 1, your projects and tasks you are actively committed to accomplishing
Index (BuJo)	Your journal's Table of Contents that points to the pages of your various lists/collections (e.g., Horizons, Monthly Log/Calendar, Today)
Log (BuJo)	The "journaling" part of the Bullet Journal Method where you are actively logging/writing about the topic of that Log. For example, your Today/Daily Log, Monthly Log, Financial/Spending Log, etc.

Rapid Logging (BuJo)	The BuJo Method of quickly annotating thoughts and status of activities with various symbols
Workflow (GTD)	There are two major Workflows in GTD: The GTD Workflow® which can be applied at each Horizon. It involves Capturing, Clarifying, Organizing, Reflecting, and Engaging. The second workflow involves your Inboxes and "turning things into what they are"; each item will end up either (or a combination of) something to do/defer/delegate/incubate, an appointment, a contact, project support or reference material, or trash.

HELPFUL RESOURCES

Help With Habits and Productivity

Building Productive Habits https://gtd-with.com/Habits

Emptying Your Inbox https://gtd-with.com/EmptyInbox

Personal Productivity Club https://gtd-with.com/PPC

Learn More About David Allen and Ryder Carroll

David Allen's Author Page https://gtd-with.com/DavidAllen

The Official Getting Things Done Website https://gtd-with.com/GTD

GTD on YouTube https://gtd-with.com/YouTubeGTD

BulletJournal.com https://gtd-with.com/BulletJournal

BuJo Notebook https://gtd-with.com/BuJo

Supplies and Accessories

Folding Ruler https://gtd-with.com/FoldingRuler

Journaling Highlighters https://gtd-with.com/Highlighters

Colored Pens and Pencils https://gtd-with.com/PensAndPencils

Large Pen Loops https://gtd-with.com/LargePenLoops

Narrow Pen Loops https://gtd-with.com/NarrowPenLoops

Gel Pens https://gtd-with.com/PilotG2

The Author's Website

The GTD-With Website https://gtd-with.com/

THANK YOU's

I've read it before in other books, but never truly appreciated how much support it takes from family, friends, and colleagues to write a book until I started this effort. Thank you to Linda, my long-suffering wife of 37 years, for putting up with the tinkerer in me and then, these last months, looking at my back as I powered through writing this book. What a loving companion and best friend! Many thanks to Xenia Ferraro of the Productive Space Design Co. (Learn more about her cool services here: http://www.productivespacedesignco.com). Xenia' insightful feedback, proof reading, and all around cheerleading me in this effort were a godsend. Finally, thank you to the like-minded colleagues in the Personal Productivity Club who are always striving to stay focused and productive (without losing their sense of humor!). Thank you everyone; without you in my life, this couldn't have been possible.

ABOUT THE AUTHOR

Derek Reinhard's professional career spans decades of productivity in various styles—from the old productivity card folios of the 1980's when he was a mainframe computer operator, to checklists and time management during his 20-years serving in the United States Air Force as a pilot and staff officer, and on to the early days of productivity systems with Franklin-Covey and David Allen. His curiosity and passion for all anything doing with efficiency keeps him experimenting and improving on being his best and most effective. His love of teaching has kept him involved in anything doing with sharing his knowledge; he was an instructor pilot in fighters and basic fast-jets early in his USAF career, and then went on be a certified Franklin-Covey instructor for two organizations he worked for; then most recently designing and delivering instructional sessions for the Department of Veterans Affairs in Washington, DC. Derek and his wife, Linda, live in Northern Virginia.

Printed in Great Britain
by Amazon